4865

BLEVINS ELEMENTARY LIBRARY

Birthdays Around the World

Celebrating Birthdays in Australia

by Cheryl L. Enderlein

Content Consultants

Michael K. Corbitt
Principal Librarian
Embassy of Australia

Justine Lovett
American Australian Association

Hilltop Books

An Imprint of Franklin Watts
A Division of Grolier Publishing
New York   London   Hong Kong   Sydney
Danbury, Connecticut

Hilltop Books
http://publishing.grolier.com
Copyright © 1998 by Capstone Press. All rights reserved.
No part of this book may be reproduced without written permission from the publisher. The publisher takes no responsibility for the use of any of the materials or methods described in this book, nor for the products thereof.
Published simultaneously in Canada.
Printed in the United States of America.

Library of Congress Cataloging-in-Publication Data
Enderlein, Cheryl L.
    Celebrating birthdays in Australia/by Cheryl L. Enderlein.
      p. cm.--(Birthdays around the world)
    Includes bibliographical references (p. 23) and index.
    Summary: Discusses the parties, decorations, food, music, games, and presents found at Australian birthday celebrations.
    ISBN 1-56065-759-6
    1. Birthdays--Juvenile literature. 2. Children's parties--Australia--Juvenile literature. 3. Australia--Social life and customs--Juvenile literature. [1. Birthdays. 2. Parties. 3. Australia--Social life and customs.] I. Title. II. Series.
    GV1472.7.B5E52   1998
    394.2--dc21

                                    97-44681
                                      CIP
                                       AC

Editorial credits
Editor, Mark Drew; additional editing, Colleen Sexton; cover design, Timothy Halldin;
  photo research, Michelle L. Norstad

Photo credits
Australasian Photographic Imaging/Karl Fehr, cover, 6, 8, 10, 12, 14, 16, 18
Australian Embassy, 4
Unicorn Stock Photos/Frank Pennington, 20

Table of Contents

Facts about Australia 5
What Is a Birthday? 7
Birthday Parties 9
Decorations 11
Food 13
Music 15
Presents 17
Turning 21 19
Aboriginal Traditions 21
Hands On: Make Fairy Bread 22
Words to Know 23
Read More 23
Useful Addresses 24
Internet Sites 24
Index 24

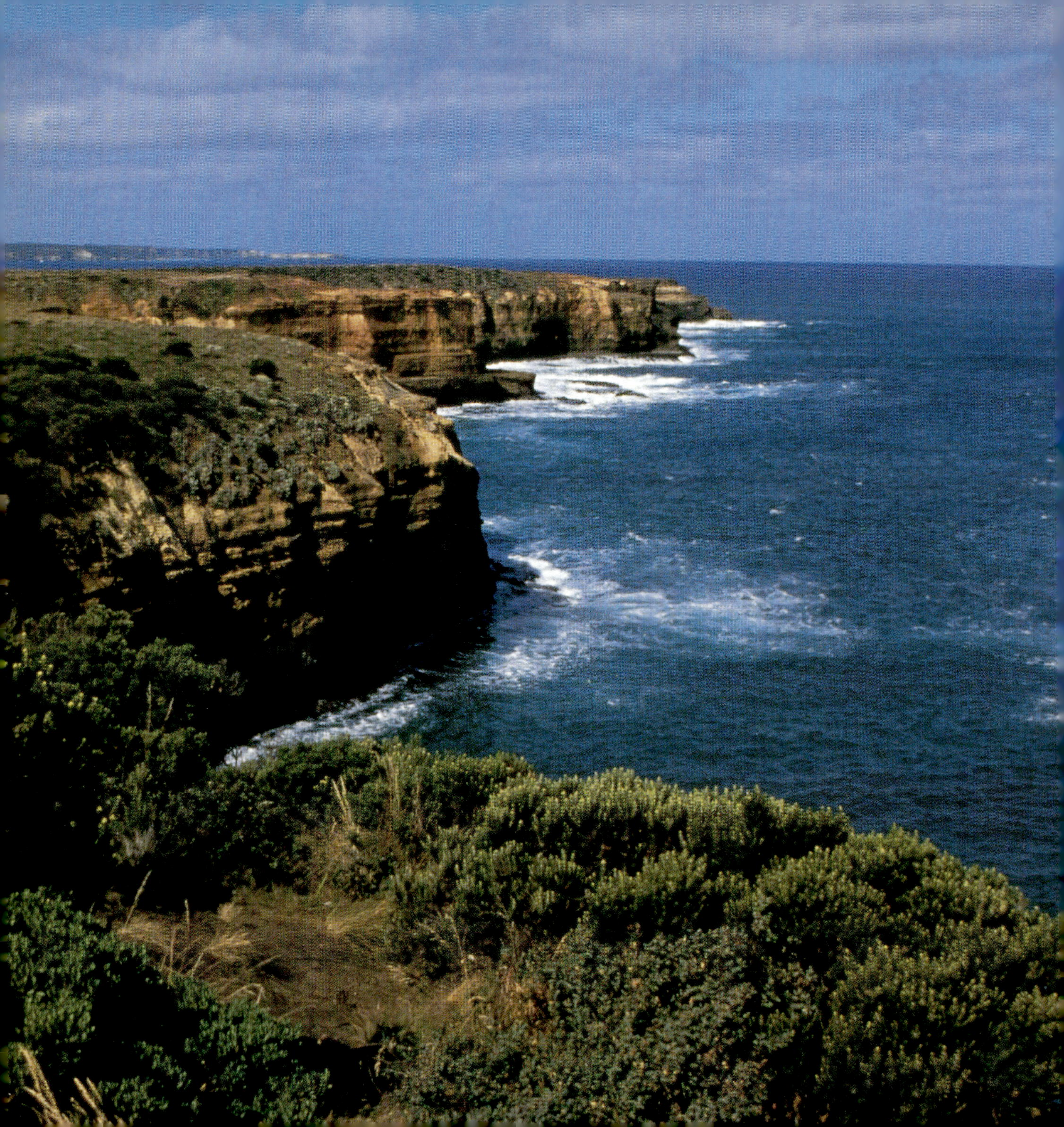

Facts about Australia

Australia is the largest island in the world. It is almost as big as the United States.

Australia is also the smallest continent. A continent is a large area of land. There are seven continents in the world. The other continents are Africa, Antarctica, Asia, Europe, North America, and South America.

Australia is in the southern half of the world. The word Australia means southern. Australia lies between the Indian Ocean and the Pacific Ocean.

People from Australia are called Australians or Aussies. They speak English. Australians come from many backgrounds. Most Australians have British or Irish backgrounds.

Many Aboriginals live in Australia. The Aboriginals were the first people to live in Australia. They settled the land thousands of years ago.

Australia is the largest island in the world.

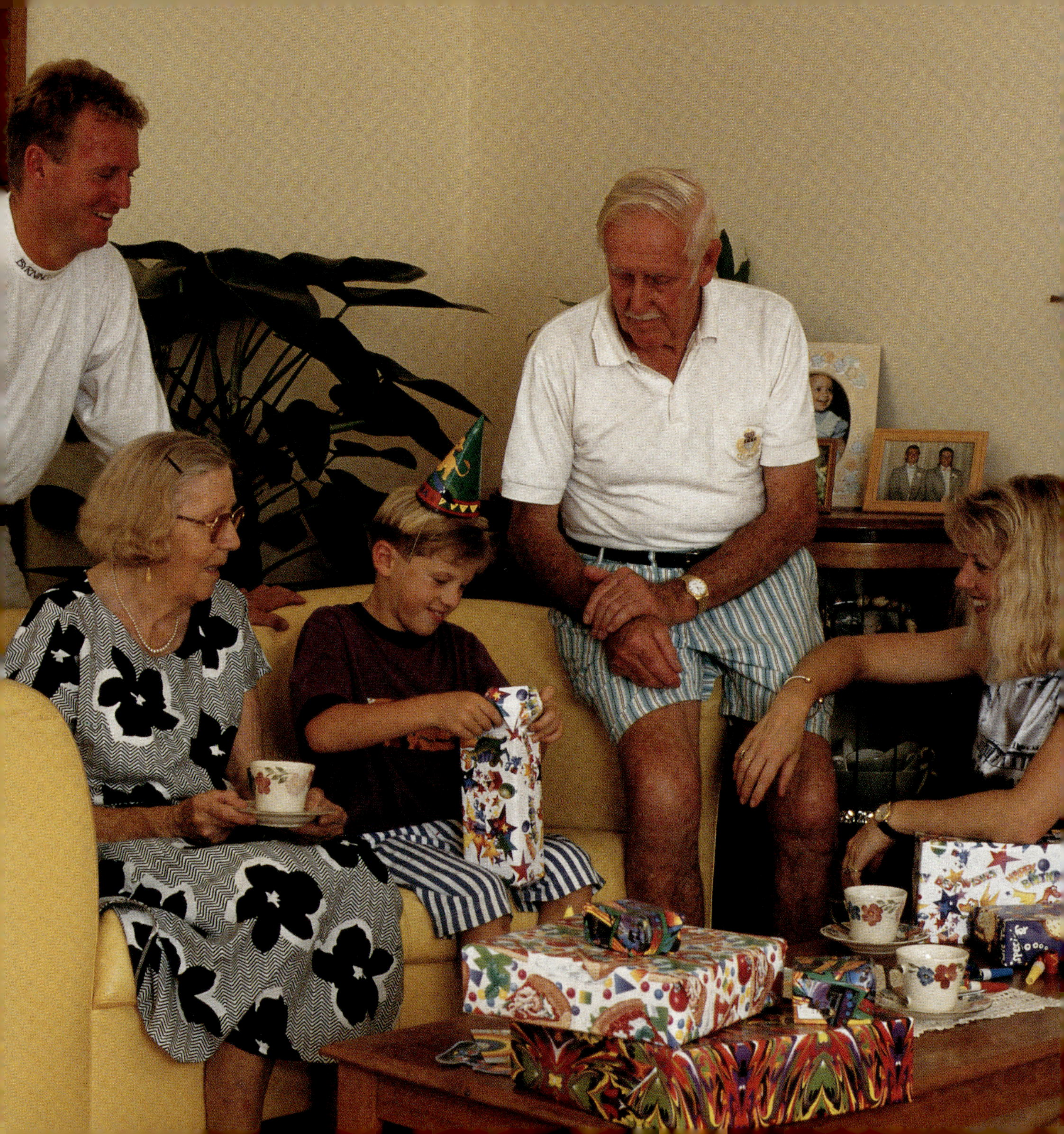

What Is a Birthday?

A birthday is the day a person was born. People celebrate their birthdays once each year. Celebrate means to do something fun on a special occasion.

A birthday is like a measuring stick. A birthday measures a person's age. A person is one year older each time he or she has a birthday.

Some families have birthday traditions. A tradition is something people have done for many years. Grandparents pass traditions to parents. Parents pass traditions to children.

Giving presents is a common birthday tradition. Celebrating birthdays with family and friends is also a popular tradition.

Giving presents is a common birthday tradition.

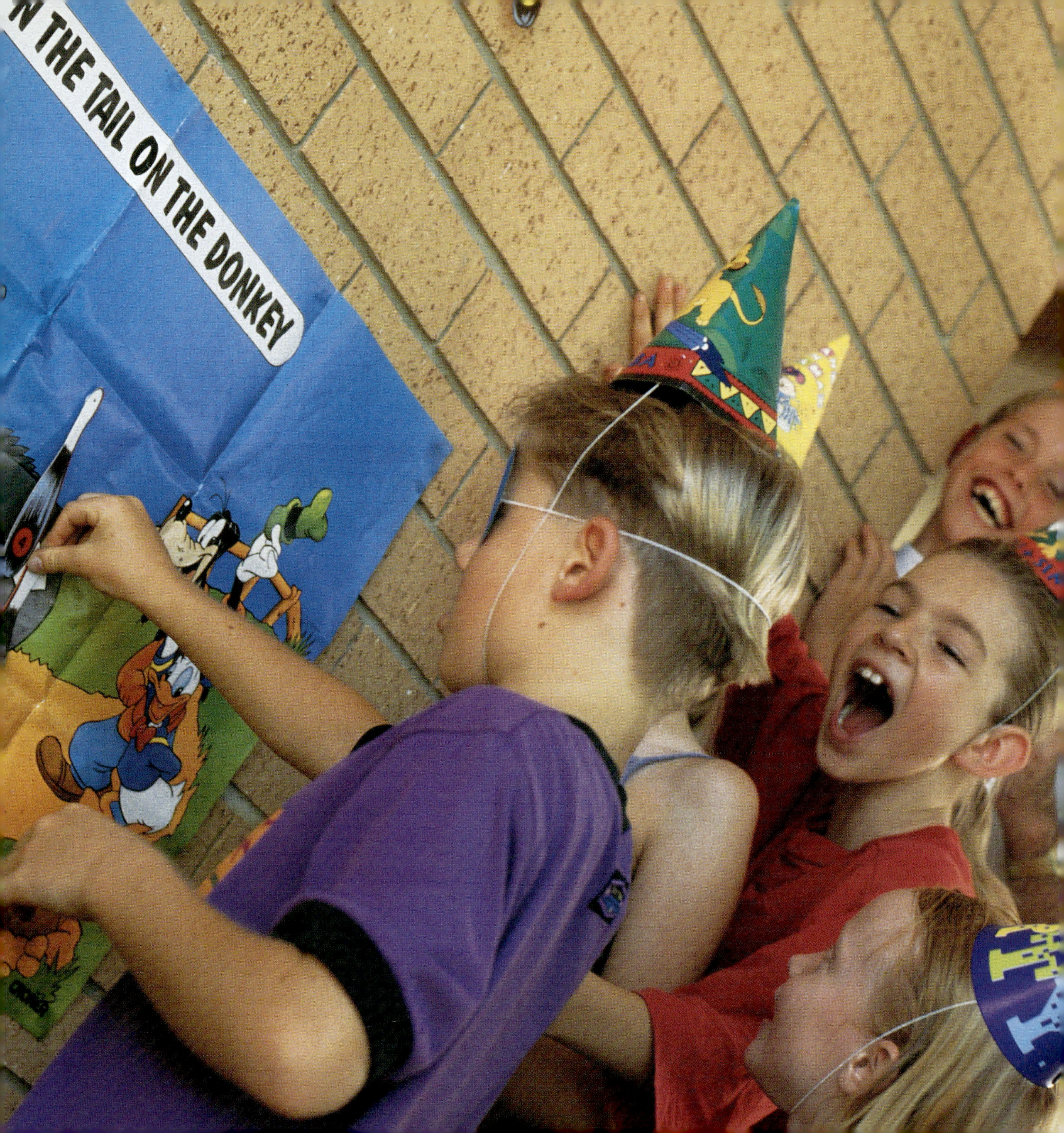
THE TAIL ON THE DONKEY

Birthday Parties

One way to celebrate a birthday is to have a party. Most Australian birthday parties take place in the birthday person's house or yard.

Family members plan the party. They help decide what to do and what to eat. They pick food and games the birthday person likes best.

The birthday person invites people to help celebrate. Invite means to ask people to come. Children in Australia invite friends and family members to birthday parties. The birthday person buys or makes invitations. Then the birthday person sends the invitations.

People who come to the party are called guests. Guests come to eat and play games. Two games Australian children play are musical chairs and pin the tail on the donkey.

Guests play games at birthday parties in Australia.

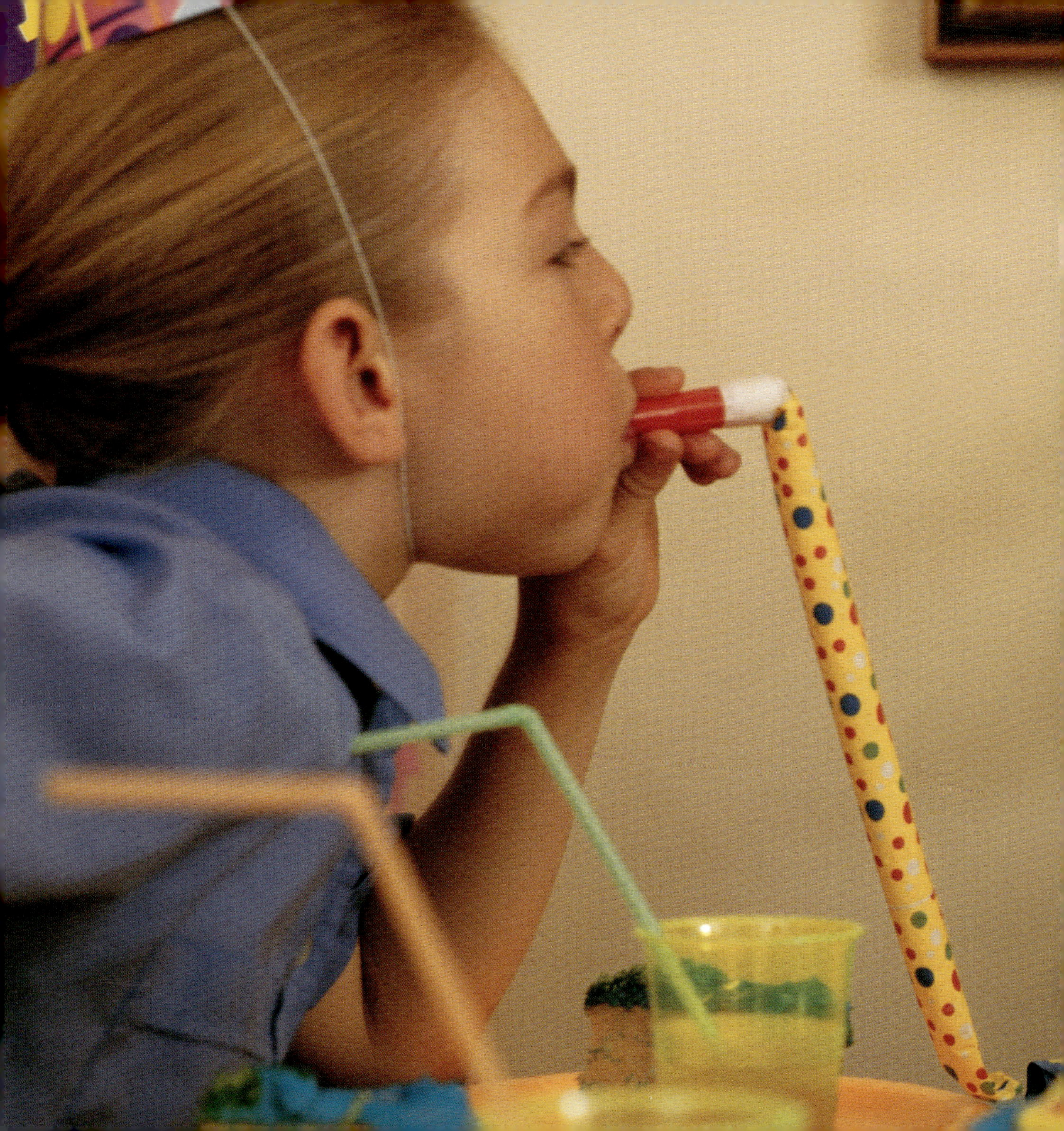

Decorations

Family members decorate for the party. They blow up balloons and hang streamers. Streamers are long, thin pieces of paper. The balloons and streamers are colorful. The family serves food on colorful dishes.

The birthday person sits at the head of the table. The head of the table is a place of honor. The family may decorate the birthday person's chair.

The guests at the party wear pointed hats. Sometimes they wear masks. They blow into noisemakers. A noisemaker is made of curled-up paper. It uncurls and makes noise when a person blows into it.

Party guests blow into noisemakers.

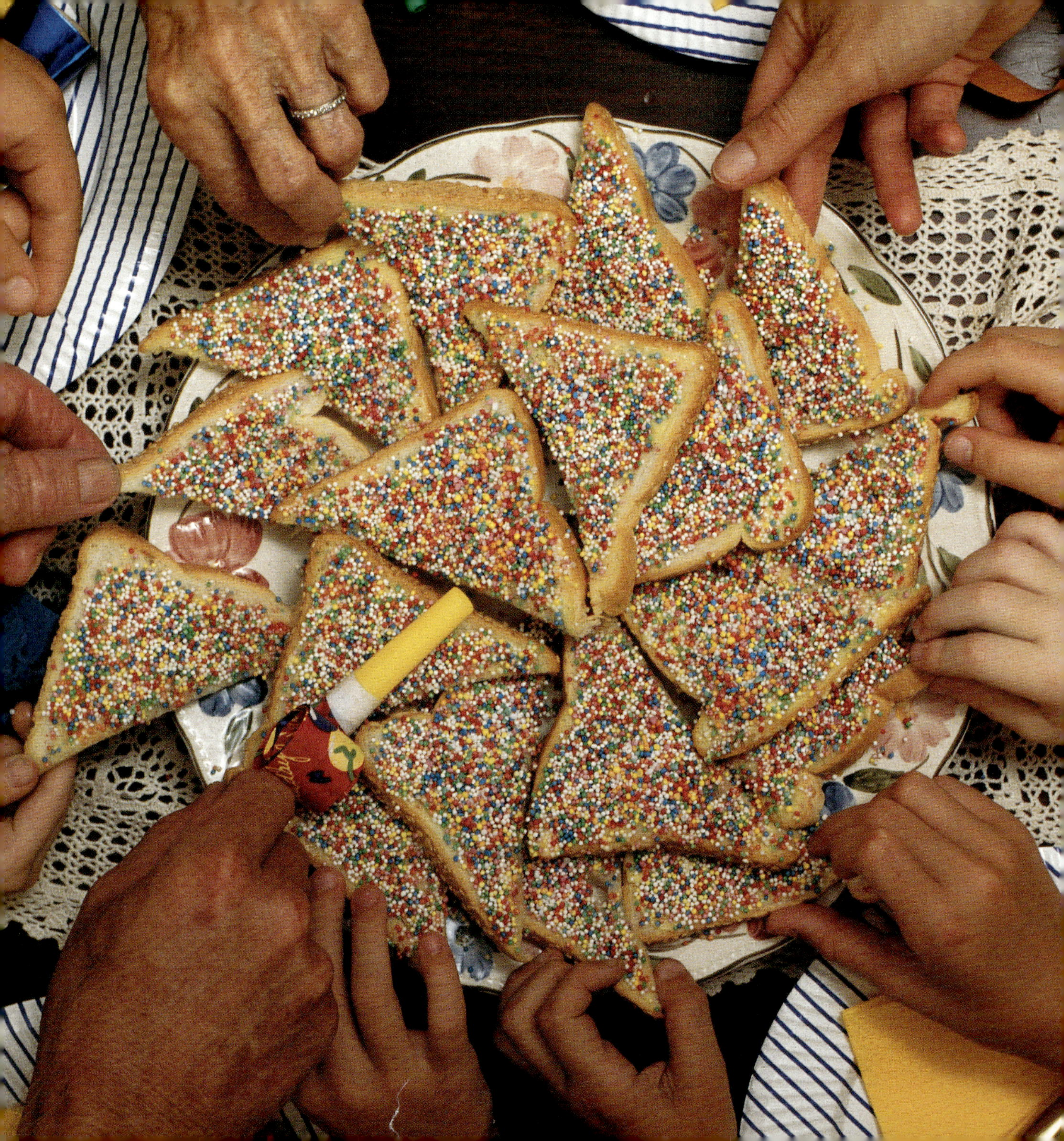

Food

Australian families serve finger foods at birthday parties. Finger foods are foods people can eat with their fingers.

One finger food Australian families serve is small hot dogs. Australians call these hot dogs franks or saveloys. They also serve tiny meat pies and cheese snacks. Cheese snacks are yellow chips shaped like rings. People wear the cheese snacks on their fingers for fun. Then they eat the cheese snacks.

Australian families also serve sweets at birthday parties. Lamingtons are squares of sponge cake. They are dipped in chocolate and rolled in coconut. Chocolate crackles are balls of crispy rice cereal covered with chocolate. Fairy bread is buttered bread with candy sprinkles on top. Guests also eat ice cream and birthday cake.

People eat fairy bread at Australian birthday parties.

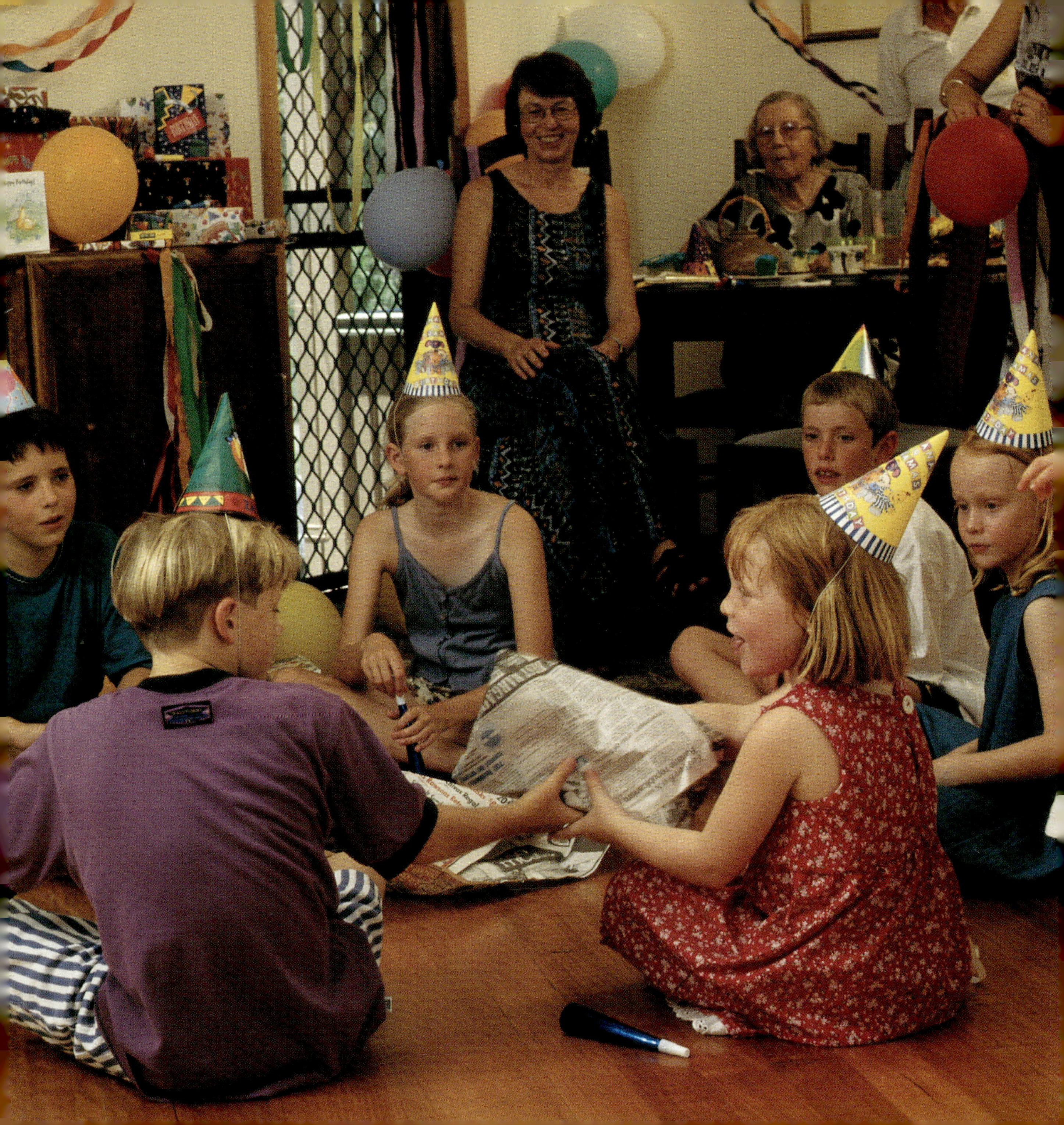

Music

The guests sing when the family brings out the birthday cake. They sing the happy birthday song. It is the same one sung in North America. The guests also count the age of the birthday person. They count out loud and clap once for each year. Then they add one more clap for good luck.

Children in Australia play a musical game called pass the parcel. A parcel is a wrapped present. An adult wraps a small present in many layers of paper. The guests do not know what is in the parcel.

The children sit in a circle. They pass the parcel around the circle while music plays. Then the music stops. The person holding the parcel unwraps one layer of paper. The music starts again. The children keep doing this. The person who unwraps the final layer is lucky. That person gets to keep the present.

Australian children play a musical game called pass the parcel.

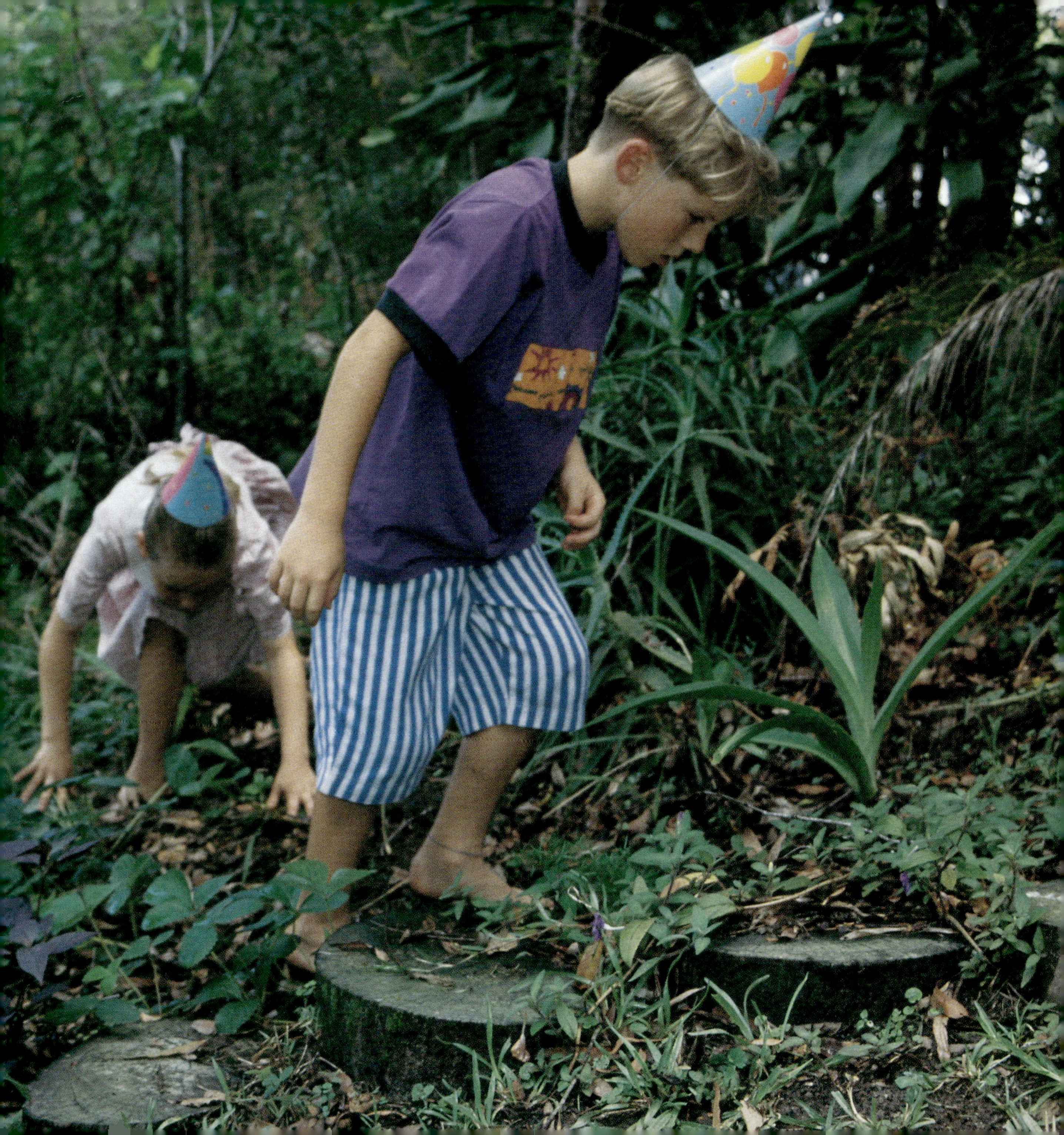

Presents

Guests bring presents to a birthday party. They go shopping to buy the presents. They pick out things they think the birthday person would like. They often pick toys, books, or games.

Guests wrap the presents in birthday paper. They may put bows on top of the presents. Guests sometimes include handmade birthday cards with presents.

The birthday person opens the presents during the party. Then the birthday person gives each guest a bag of lollies. Lollies are candy. This is how the birthday person thanks the guests.

There are many kinds of candy in each bag. Sometimes guests must hunt for their bags of lollies. The guests save their lollies to take home after the party.

Sometimes guests must hunt for their bags of lollies.

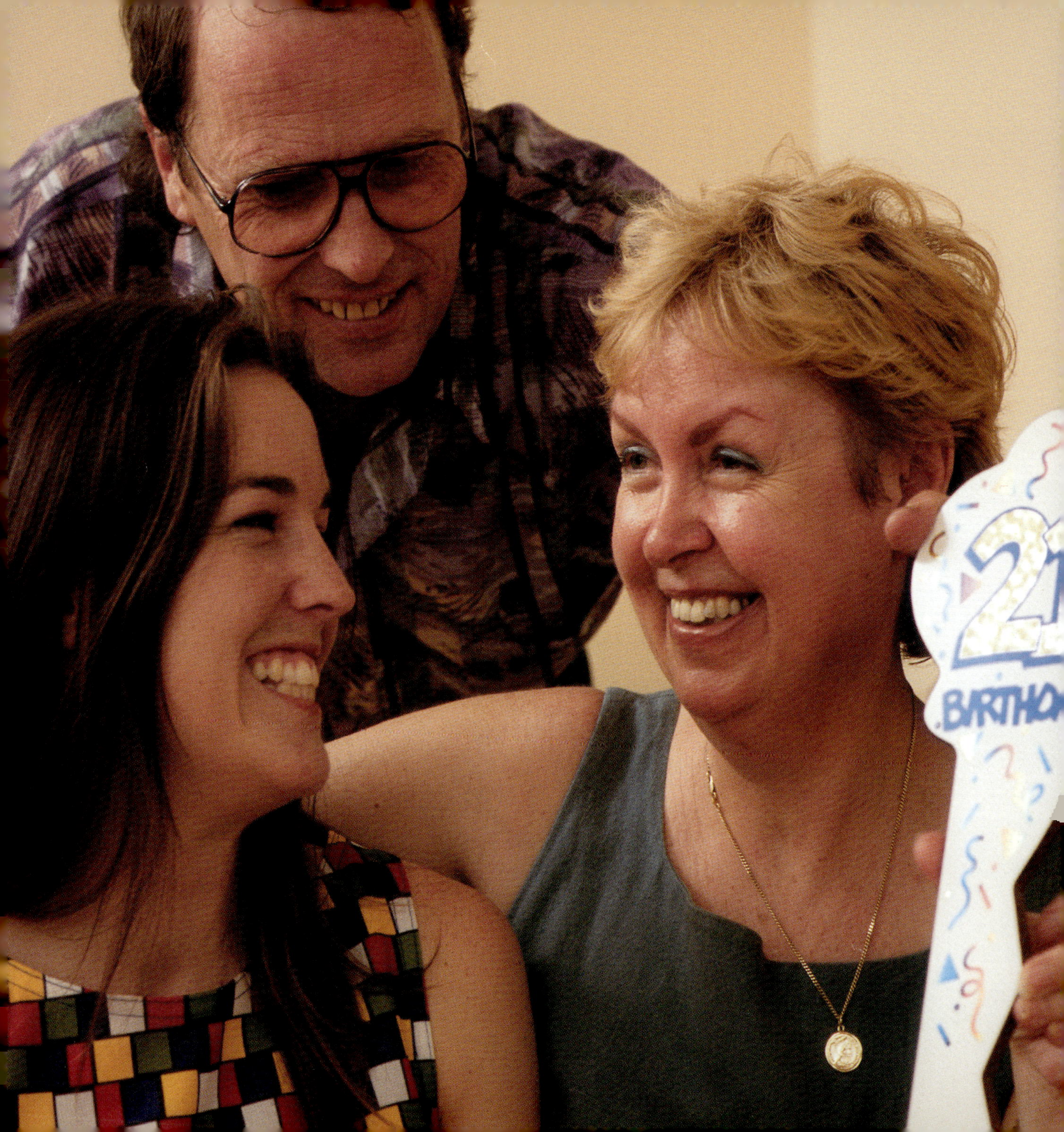

Turning 21

Countries often have birthday traditions. Turning 21 is special in Australia. Australians call this a coming of age birthday.

The parents of the birthday person have a party. It is called a key to the house party. Parents give the birthday person a big key. They buy the key or make it out of cardboard. They cover the cardboard with silver paper.

The key stands for independence. Independence means living without help from other people. Guests at the party give the birthday person keys, too.

Turning 21 is special in Australia.

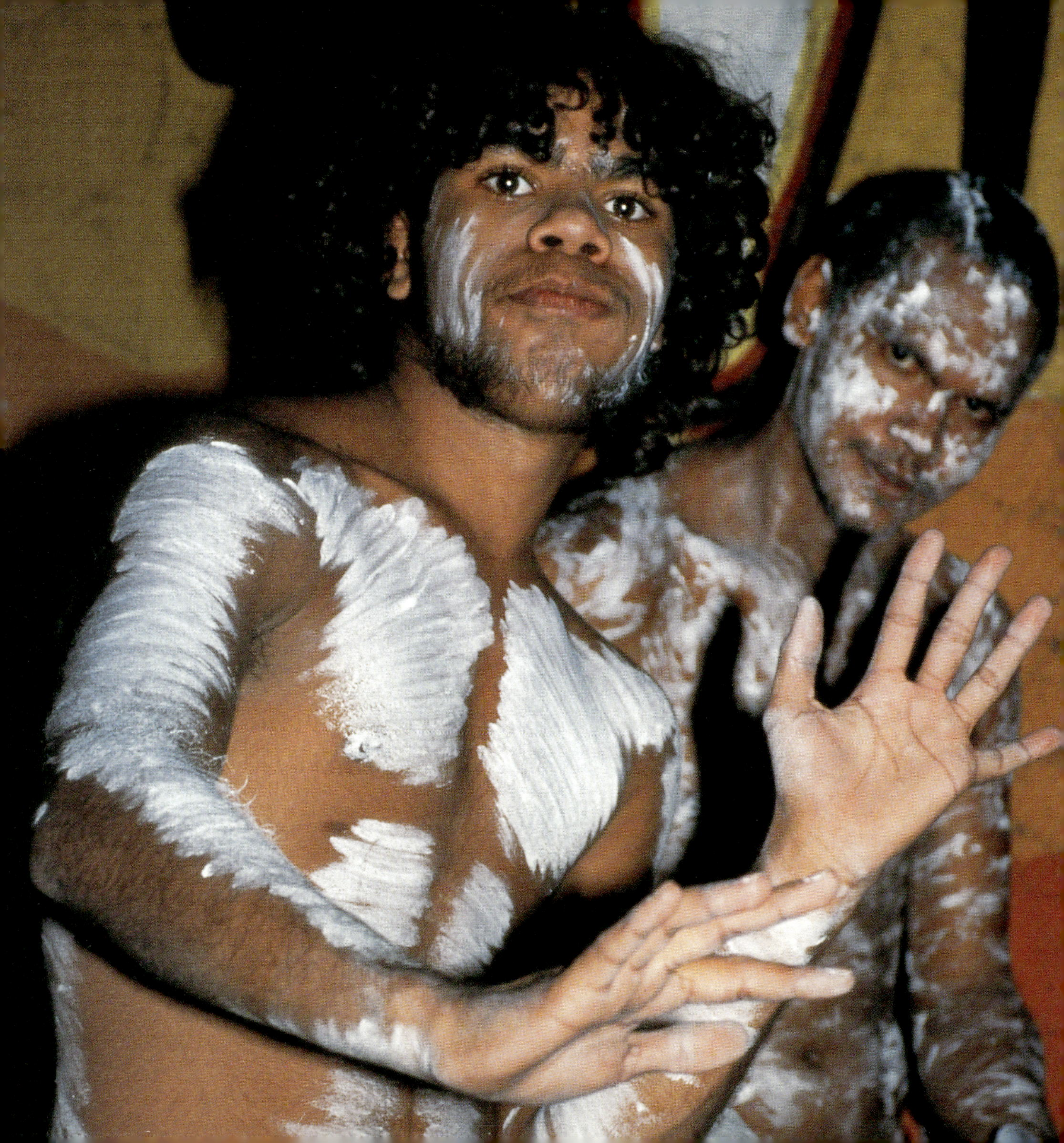

Aboriginal Traditions

There are more than 500 Aboriginal tribes in Australia. Each tribe has its own traditions. Some Aboriginal tribes have practiced their traditions for thousands of years.

Many Aboriginal tribes have coming of age ceremonies. Coming of age means becoming an adult. A ceremony is a set of words and actions.

Young people learn about family members during the ceremony. They also learn about the history of their tribes.

Aboriginal tribes celebrate coming of age in many ways. The young people may paint shapes on their faces and bodies. They may wear special clothes. They might speak, sing, or dance during the ceremony.

Aboriginals may paint their bodies for a coming of age ceremony.

Hands On: Make Fairy Bread

Guests eat fairy bread at Australian birthday parties. You can make fairy bread.

What You Need

1 slice of white bread
Butter or margarine
1 sharp knife

1 jar of colored sprinkles
1 butter knife
1 napkin or plate

What You Do

1. Let the butter or margarine soften.
2. Use the butter knife to butter one slice of bread. Spread butter on only one side.
3. Shake the jar of sprinkles over the buttered bread. Keep shaking until the bread is covered.
4. Ask an adult to cut the bread from corner to corner in both directions. Now you have four triangle shapes.
5. Put the pieces on a napkin or plate.
6. Serve fairy bread to your family or friends.

Words to Know

celebrate (SEHL-uh-brayt)—to do something fun on a special occasion
ceremony (SER-uh-moh-nee)—a set of words and actions
guest (GEST)—a person who comes to a party
independence (in-di-PEN-duhnss)—living without help from other people
invite (in-VITE)—to ask people to come
parcel (PAR-suhl)—a wrapped package or present
streamer (STREE-mur)—a long, thin piece of colored paper
tradition (truh-DISH-uhn)—something people have done for many years

Read More

Arnold, Helen. *Australia*. Austin, Tex.: Raintree Steck-Vaughn, 1995.
Bickman, Connie. *Children of Australia*. Through the Eyes of Children. Minneapolis: Abdo and Daughters, 1994.
Dahl, Michael. *Australia*. Countries of the World. Mankato, Minn.: Bridgestone Books, 1997.
Feldman, Eve B. *Birthdays!: Celebrating Life Around the World*. Mahwah, N.J.: Bridgewater Books, 1996.

Useful Addresses

American Australian Association
750 Lexington Ave., 17th Floor
New York, NY 10022

Embassy of Australia
1601 Massachusetts Ave. NW
Washington, DC 20036-2273

Internet Sites

About Australia
http://www.about-australia.com
Kids Parties Connection
http://kidsparties.com

Index

Aboriginal, 5, 21
balloons, 11
cake, 13, 15
ceremony, 21
chocolate crackles, 13
coming of age, 19, 21
decorations, 11
fairy bread, 13
guest, 9, 11, 15, 17, 19

independence, 19
invitation, 9
key, 19
lollies, 17
noisemaker, 11
party, 9, 11, 13, 17, 19
presents, 7, 15, 17
streamers, 11
tradition, 7, 19, 21